FOLK

/ FŌK /

noun: used as a friendly form
of address to a group of people

adjective: of or relating
to the traditional art or culture
of a community

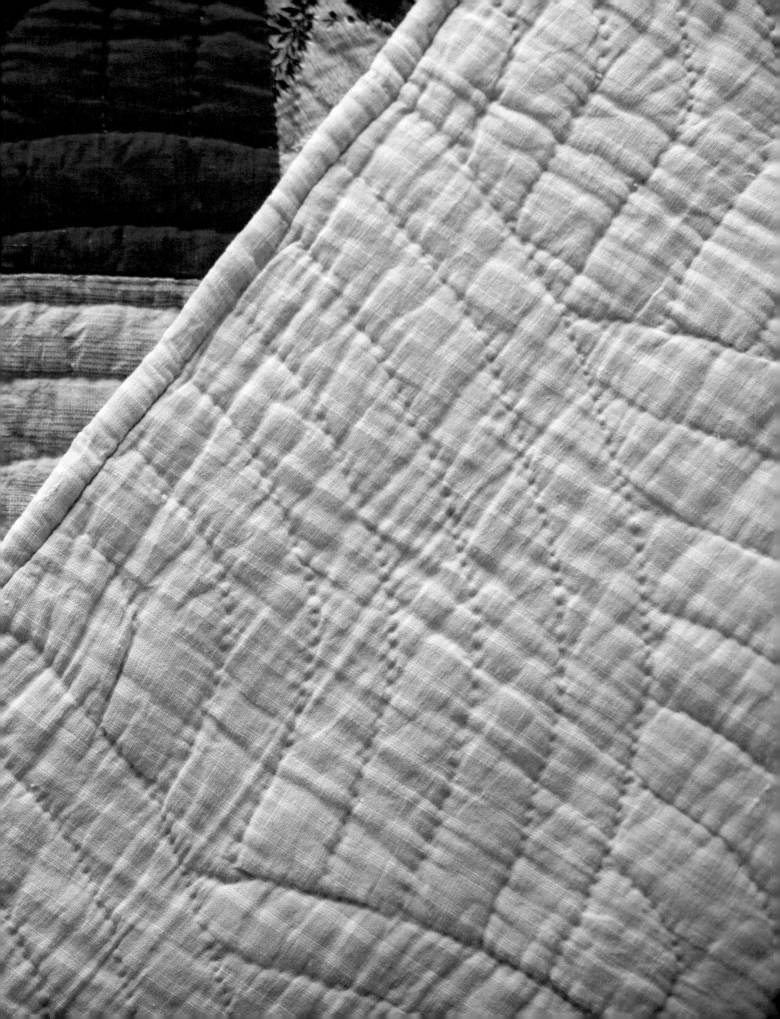

Quiltfolk

PUBLISHER *Michael McCormick*

EDITOR IN CHIEF *Mary Fons*

CREATIVE DIRECTOR *Janelle Frazier*

BRAND DIRECTOR *Riane Menardi Morrison*

COPY EDITOR *Mary Kate Karr-Petras*

PHOTOGRAPHERS
Azuree Wiitala
Melanie Zacek

CONTRIBUTING WRITERS
Meg Cox
Kestrel Michaud

GUEST CONTRIBUTORS
Lindsey Hatfield
Pamela Reed

Quiltfolk is a community-supported quarterly.
Visit Quiltfolk.com.

SUBMISSIONS
submit@quiltfolk.com

QUESTIONS
hello@quiltfolk.com

 /quiltfolk   @quiltfolk   @quiltfolk

PO Box 10796, Eugene, OR 97440
Quiltfolk.com

OPPOSITE: At the first-ever Quiltfolk show-and-tell, Diana Pargeon brought this exquisite Crazy quilt made by her great grandmother in 1883.
PREVIOUS PAGE: Detail, late 1800s patchwork quilt from the Hunsaker-Morrison collection at the Clark County Museum in Henderson, Nevada.

Start to finish, it takes us about nine months to make an issue of *Quiltfolk*.

The lead time means we effectively work in the future, since the magazine content we're making at any given moment won't exist in print for another nine months. As such, we avoid including in our stories information about "upcoming" events like shop-hops or exhibits, since most will have come and gone by the time the issue comes out. We're also careful not to reference current events in the magazine; whatever the news might be while we're creating the next issue of *Quiltfolk*, it'll be ancient history by the time readers hold the finished product.

I've agonized over this issue's letter, trying to write around what's happening, but I can't.

It's the middle of April. I'm at home. It's been raining all day. Out my window, the Chicago I love looks so different than it did "before": before the pandemic, before quarantines, before so much economic uncertainty. Before the world turned upside down.

Like me, you've probably thought a lot about what life was like "before." We went to games and ate at restaurants; there weren't lines outside the grocery store; we were sewing patchwork, not face masks. I think about those things, too. But there's something else I'll always think of when I remember "before."

I'll think of Nevada.

The girls and I spent 12 days traversing this spectacular state to collect the stories you're about to read. As road trips go, it was classic *Quiltfolk*: We high-fived; we passed french fries around in the car; we nudged each other to look out the window, this time at Nevada's snowcapped mountains, the sand dunes that rippled across the desert, three wild horses grazing on a roadside hill. We squeezed through crowds in Las Vegas, took selfies with showgirls, and at *Quiltfolk's* first-ever show-and-tell event, we hugged dozens of quilters. In a word, we were *together*, and the backdrop for that togetherness was Nevada in all her feather-boa'ed, blue-sky finery. Could there be a better "before" than that?

I hope by the time you read this, many months from now, we can all be back on the open road. Whether we are or not — you have more information than I do right now — I promise you, we'll always have Nevada.

xoxo,

Mary Fons
EDITOR IN CHIEF

Quiltfolk

ISSUE

15

THIS PAGE: Retired casino and nightclub signage laid to rest at the Neon Museum in Las Vegas. **ON THE COVER:** Lone Star made by Mabel Viola Meador, ca. 1930. **BACK COVER:** A LeMoyne Star quilt (ca. 1860) from professor Colleen Hall-Patton's personal collection.

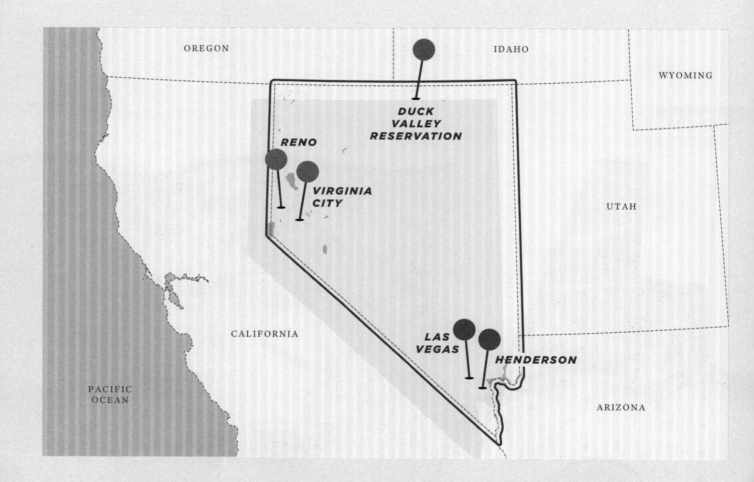

ISSUE

15 | *Nevada*

Quiltfolk knows that wherever we roam, we'll find surprises and uncover a state's best-kept secrets. But in Virginia City, one quiltmaker told us that the whole *state* of Nevada is America's best-kept secret. By the time our trip was over, we agreed.

We expected that we would meet fascinating people, but we didn't expect to see wild horses grazing on hillsides, which we did — twice. We knew we'd get great views of the desert, but we didn't count on snowcapped mountains. Of course everyone was excited for Las Vegas, but none of us could know that walking on a white-sand playa under a brilliant blue sky would be even more fun than enjoying a cocktail (or two) on the Strip.

Though gaming cities Las Vegas and Reno draw millions of thrill-seekers to the state every year, Nevada also calls those looking for a particular kind of serenity only found in the Southwest. The whole population of the Silver State (a reference to its once-central role in American mining) is barely over 3 million; with 110,000 square miles, that gives a person a lot of breathing room.

Every day of our Nevada trip held surprise and delight, and we've done our very best to bring our happy discoveries to you in Issue 15. Along with so many others, you'll meet a young woman who wears her patchwork on her sleeve; get to know a group of big kids making quilts for little ones; and attend the first-ever *Quiltfolk* show-and-tell, where more than 40 quilters weren't shy about spilling the beans on what makes Nevada so great.

NORTHERN NEVADA

Take To The Sky

NORTHERN NEVADA

ARE YOU A POET OR A NOVELIST looking to relocate? Are you seeking a place as intense and dramatic as you are? Do you have a car that gets good gas mileage? If you answered yes to these questions, you're the perfect candidate for relocation to Northern Nevada, a place with enough intrigue to inspire a masterpiece.

With miles and miles of what feels like endless rangeland — drivers are advised to beware of cow crossings — and large tracts of protected tribal land, Nevada's sweeping northern half is so sparsely populated, the openness can make a person feel suspiciously small. Tiny towns are few and far between, so those passing through would be well-advised to fill up the tank and stock provisions before heading out.

But this tension is what makes the upper part of Nevada so electric and inspiring to those who can contend with it. Here, skies are infinite and pastel; the temperature fluctuates wildly from day to night and from elevation to elevation. Up here, you're closer to Tahoe and the Sierra Nevada mountains than you are to Las Vegas (which many locals consider a huge plus).

Poets and writers who find this environment fascinating would say the same of the people who live here. We met an entire school full of extraordinary youth, a real-life fire goddess, and a frontier woman whose patchwork garments find a place in big cities.

BY **Riane Menardi Morrison**

The Second Life
OF SARAH LILLEGARD

As US 395 stretches its way north from Reno, the landscape shifts from neon lights and casinos to rolling hills, tall grasses, and sagebrush. About 45 minutes out of town is a small but sturdy homestead, situated humbly on three-and-a-half acres of land. It was settled in the early 1800s, and over time, the many hands of those who have lived here have shaped the property and the land around it into a home.

Today, the place still evokes its earliest homestead days. There's a small, one-room cabin with an earth-berm floor and cement walls built entirely by hand 40 years ago. "His" and "hers" outhouses serve as plumbing for the current occupants. Dirt paths lined with desert plants wind their way between structures on the property: a pottery studio, a wood-fired kiln, a greenhouse. And up the hill, behind the cabin, is a small fiber studio where you'll find Sarah Lillegard quietly sewing.

Sarah Lillegard uses reclaimed textiles to stitch magic and meaning.

ABOVE, L-R: Lillegard created a jacket with Log Cabin patchwork as part of her 2020 "Hearth" collection; Lillegard incorporated Flying Geese at the yoke of this jacket to imply "drawing up your shoulders for a shrug or bracing breath." **OPPOSITE:** Lillegard and partner Casey Clark.

Lillegard and her partner, potter Casey Clark, have lived on this property for about a year. Before they started their second life, they lived in Reno, where the two artists shared a studio space and were active in the local arts community.

Though she practices embroidery and weaving, Lillegard is best known for her hand-crafted denim jackets, the backs of which incorporate traditional patchwork worked in a contemporary style.

"I love jean jackets," Lillegard said, "because I feel like they're a universal garment. Different people of different cliques wear jean jackets and it resonates, whether it's a motorcycle gang, or a cowboy, or someone in an urban setting wearing it for fashion. A jean jacket, kind of like jeans themselves, is something that can jump between cultures."

Lillegard's mother, who has been sewing for more than 50 years, taught her to quilt. Over time,

fueled by an interest in the legacy of other crafts — including her partner's specialty, pottery — Lillegard became fascinated by the history of quilt patterns and quilt blocks, which shared similarities with other crafts she was passionate about.

"Pottery is one of the oldest crafts. Weaving is one of the oldest crafts. You needed vessels to drink from, you needed garments to put over yourself," she said. "And so when you start to work in them, you're actually connecting centuries of making and multiple civilizations. I feel like quilting might be similar. You can step back so far, and there are so many different narratives about how and why that pattern was made, or named, or renamed, or restructured. It feels like when you're working with it, it's not in isolation. It's like tapping into a legacy of making, which," Lillegard said with a smile, "has some mojo magic to it."

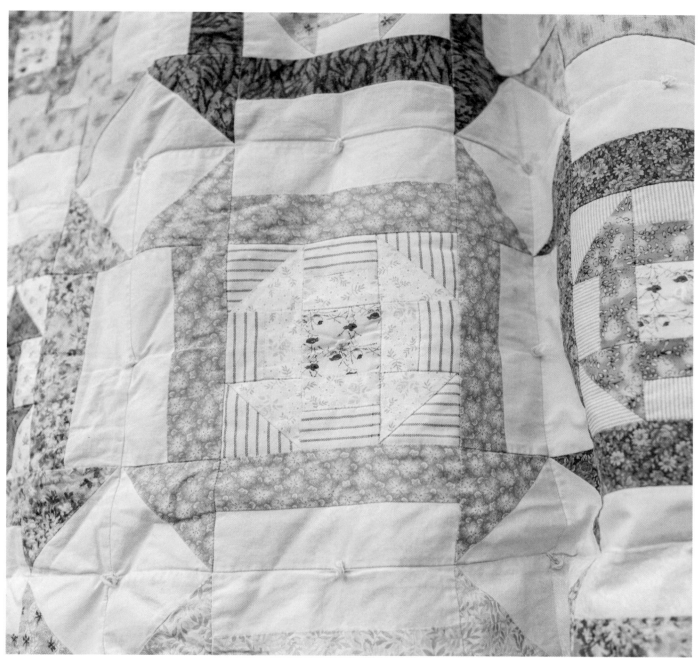

ABOVE: Detail, a Double Monkey Wrench quilt Lillegard made in 2016 with her mother, Arlene. **OPPOSITE:** The kiln, built in the ancient Japanese *anagama* or "cave kiln" style, runs just twice a year and requires a crew to stoke the flames for three days to reach the necessary temperature.

ABOVE: Scraps get a second life in the studio. OPPOSITE: Lillegard is okay with inconsistencies in the material she uses, saying: "I can mend them, but I'm perfectly happy with all the holes."

Most of Lillegard's materials are repurposed and upcycled. She scours thrift stores for denim jackets, and her friends help her look. She saves scraps of fabric from other projects, and salvages remnants from old jeans and clothing. As she works, the scraps and the jackets are reincarnated, transformed from discarded objects into wearable art.

"I'm interested in the second life of quilts, the second life of the garment," Lillegard said. "The delightful problem to solve is getting different quilt blocks on different jackets."

Lillegard carries forth the legacy of handmade by fusing tradition with modern craft. She wears her mission literally. "[A] back patch is something that designates belonging," Lillegard said. "If you're in a bowling league, you have the team name on the back. If you're part of a construction crew, it's silk-screened on the back of the shirt. So something

about us wearing our identifications on our back becomes interesting. There are these little subtleties of why you do the things you do, and that resonates."

Lillegard infuses her "second-life" philosophy not only into her craft, but also into her lifestyle, including how she and Clark see the homestead.

"There's kind of a baseline for the property," she said. "It's this question of 'What is it already doing?' Instead of saying, 'What do I want it to be?' it's like, 'What's already happening here? What's already growing? Where's the water moving? What animals are here?'"

Outside of quilting, Lillegard enjoys exploring other pursuits. She went to sheep shearing school, and shears small flocks for ranchers in the area. She teaches handwork and embroidery classes, and she writes and takes pictures for *Fibershed*, a California-based magazine.

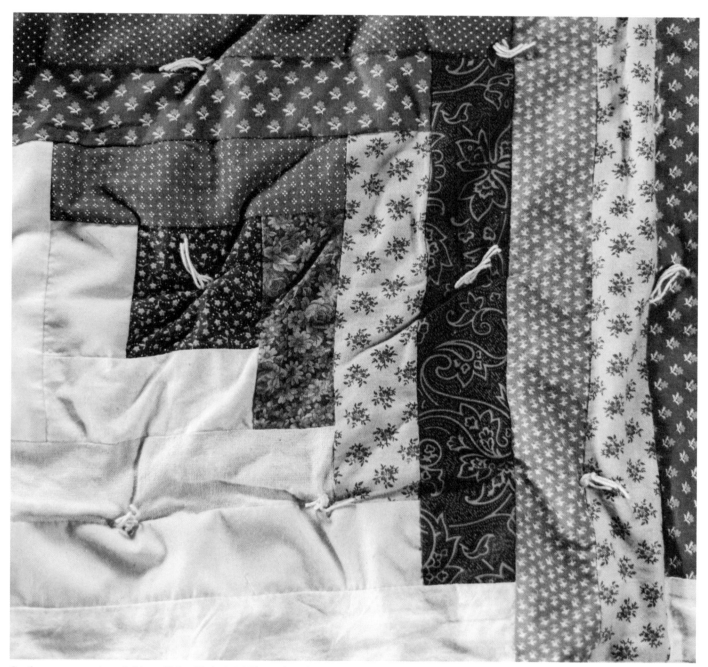

On these pages, a Log Cabin quilt for Clark that Lillegard made with help from Mom. Lillegard says her instructor insisted on proper technique: "I got a lifelong lesson in taking time to make something well — aka listening to Mom."

CLOCKWISE FROM UPPER LEFT: Yarns gifted from Reno-based weaver, spinner, and dyer Kate Hanlon; pottery for sale in the outdoor showroom; a secondhand scrap holds possibility.

At the homestead, evidence of a life lived in nature.

Though Lillegard enjoyed city life, her appreciation for nature and a rustic lifestyle runs deeper. "I really love rural communities," she said. "You have to spend some time getting to know people, [then] all this wealth of stories and history and context arises. I really like that slow reveal of rural communities. I've been an advocate of rural places for a long time, even before moving out here."

Lillegard's friends joke that her windblown, dark blonde hair matches the wild grasses that cover the land. Clark likes to tease her that their natural surroundings keep her palette "refined."

She laughed. "I'm almost obsessive," she said. "There's points where I make fun of it, that high desert palette, that subtlety of greens and browns. I'm aware that I kind of overdo it. But being in open space ... There's something about open desert. It's gratifying."

Lillegard was born in a small town south of Reno with a population of about 6,000. She went to college in Walla Walla, Washington, and after graduating landed in Reno with Clark. The couple's plan was always to return to rural life. Before they took ownership of the homestead, Clark worked with its then-owner, renowned potter Paul Herman. For 15 years, Herman was Clark's tutor and firing partner, and together they crafted pottery in the wood-fired kiln built on the property.

In 2019, Herman passed away suddenly, leaving two dogs, a cat, and a special home that needed stewarding. Clark moved from Reno to look after the property, and six months later, Lillegard wrapped up their affairs in the city and joined him.

Renowned potter Paul Herman lived on the property for 35 years; this Pinwheel quilt (date unknown) was made by his mother, Mary Herman.

ABOVE: Lillegard said of this Ocean Waves quilt made by Mary Herman, "I was cleaning the house and found it tucked away in a dresser drawer, still bright and vibrant like it had never been used." **OPPOSITE:** Dogs Cody and Tycho get in on the shot.

"We were always planning on basically doing this," Clark said. "We just anticipated being neighbors with Paul instead of taking over his property. Everything's going according to what our long-term plan was, just much faster. We thought we would have five or six years to settle in out here and slowly transition, and instead it happened almost overnight."

The gifts outweigh the challenges, he said. "It's really quiet. It's a beautiful place to live. And not having all the distractions and conveniences of town clears out a lot of your schedule so you can concentrate on making stuff, which is really a lucky privilege in a lot of ways."

It took time for Lillegard to transition back to the rural lifestyle, but now it suits her. "I was

amazed at the loneliness initially, but I think I just needed time," she said with a smile. "And now I'm perfectly happy just doing my thing, and talking to Casey at lunch, and the rest of the time talking to plants and animals."

Accustomed to their new life in the quiet desert, Lillegard and Clark are slowly transforming the property into a home that suits their worldview and their work, just as other homesteaders here have done. They're conscious of retaining the homestead's heritage — embedding themselves rather than imposing, as Lillegard would say. And amidst the stillness, Lillegard works in her studio and sews, transforming each scrap, each jacket, into something that will go on to enjoy a new, beautiful, second life.

BY **Riane Menardi Morrison**

Owyhee's Quilt Story
A SPECIAL EDUCATION

In North Central Nevada, high school students in a home economics classroom at the Owyhee Combined School are making quilt blocks. Their teacher, Pamela Reed, is a quilter and sewist who made her first quilt when she was 15, in her own high school "home ec" class. The class was supposed to be making patchwork pillows, but Reed made a queen-size quilt instead.

"I was bored!" Reed said, laughing. "I already had my pillow done. So I made a quilt in the time it took for the rest of the class to make their pillows."

Ms. Reed, as her students call her, says that today she has her dream job. After driving a semi truck for 30 years, she and her husband moved to his hometown of Owyhee seeking a more stationary life. She became a substitute teacher at the school in 2014 while pursuing her teaching certificate. As soon as she was settled, she begged the principal to open a family and consumer science class, and the principal eventually agreed.

"Until I started last year, they hadn't had home economics in 10 years," Reed said.

Home economics teacher Pamela Reed says the Owyhee school system is "like a big family, and that's what I love about it."

The Owyhee quiltmakers pose for a class picture with quilt recipients River (left) and Lucian (right) at the heart of it all.

Owyhee sits 5,400 feet above sea level within the Duck Valley Indian Reservation. The town's population sits around 1,000 and Owyhee Combined School (OCS) comprises roughly 300 students. The school teaches kindergarten through 12th grade, and nearly all of the students are members of the Shoshone-Paiute tribe.

Before taking Ms. Reed's class, most of her students had never sewn before and none of them had made a quilt. When Ms. Reed told them they would be making quilt blocks using a sewing machine, they were interested — and nervous.

"It was confusing at first; I couldn't get the hang of it," said 16-year-old Klay Thomas. He came around, though. "It's kind of interesting, taking something that's been broken down and turning it

into something new ... We have a box of scraps, and to me it's cool to turn it into something completely different."

The students learned to make blocks by sewing scraps to a newspaper foundation. As the blocks are finished, they're stored a bin. By the time the students are ready to make bigger projects (such as quilts, bags, or pillows) the bin is full of completed blocks.

One of the class's first projects was to make quilts for River and Lucian, two students in the special education program at OCS. "One of our aides who worked with River requested a quilt," said Raymond Jim, a special education teacher at Owyhee. "We thought that since we have a home ec department that makes quilts, we may as well ask."

CLOCKWISE FROM UPPER LEFT: The all-important quilt label; student Daeja says that when she's not making blocks, she's making scrunchies; outside the high school entrance.

CLOCKWISE FROM UPPER LEFT: Accumulated scraps provide material for projects; a pincushion for every student; Ms. Reed shows patriotic patchwork.

River and Lucian are all smiles in Ms. Reed's classroom. **NEXT PAGE:** River sports Nevada-appropriate footwear.

"I think it was Ms. Reed who told us we were going to make quilts for these two little guys," said Gage Johnson, 17. "So we all came together and really made them good." He pointed to a quilt on the table. "That one over there, you see all the basketballs? We made it especially for River because he loves basketball."

Alyna Teofilo, 15, and Kayla Baker, 16, are sophomores, and the class quilt project is Teofilo's first time sewing. "It taught me a lot," Teofilo said. "It inspired me to give back to people, because the quilts we made are *for* other people." The next batch of quilts will go to elders at the senior center.

"It's cool because we made them and people are

using them," Baker said. "It made me want to make more things, because now I know how."

Ms. Reed keeps her grading simple: "For one block, they get a 70 percent for the day; two blocks they get an 80 percent; three blocks they get a 90 percent; and if they make four blocks they get 100 percent," Reed said. "So it's up to them."

Mackenzie Cady, 16, is a sophomore at Owyhee. Until this year, she'd never sewn anything; now she completes four blocks every day.

"When I started doing it," she said, "it was just really fun. And it's kind of calming. I like to come into class and just sew whatever."

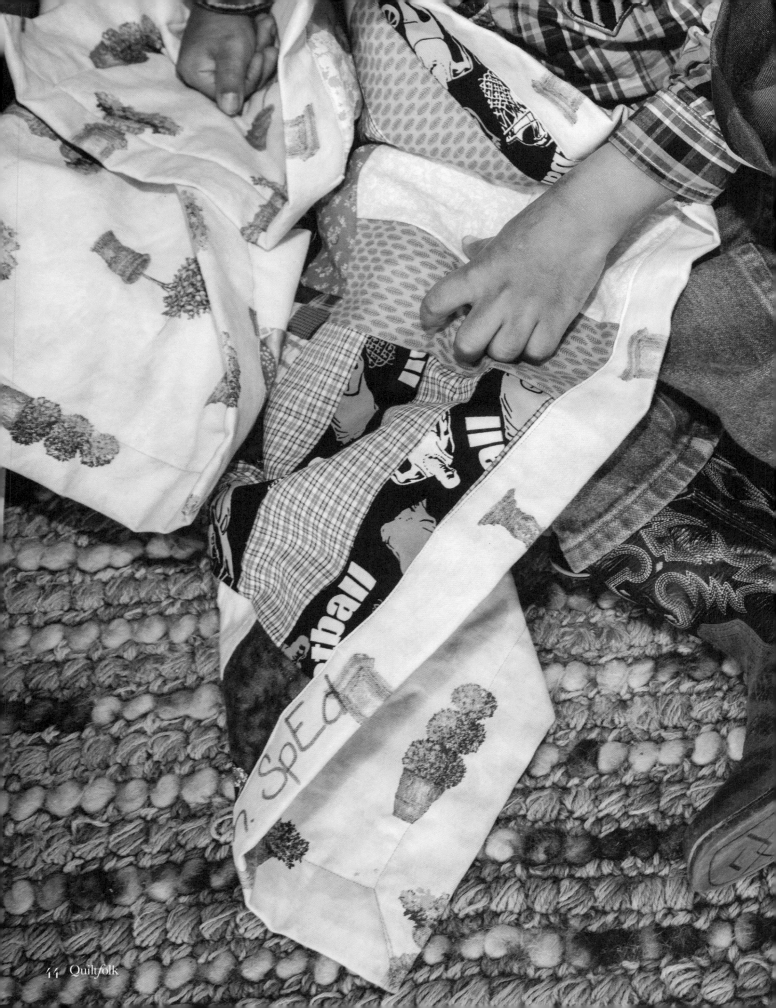

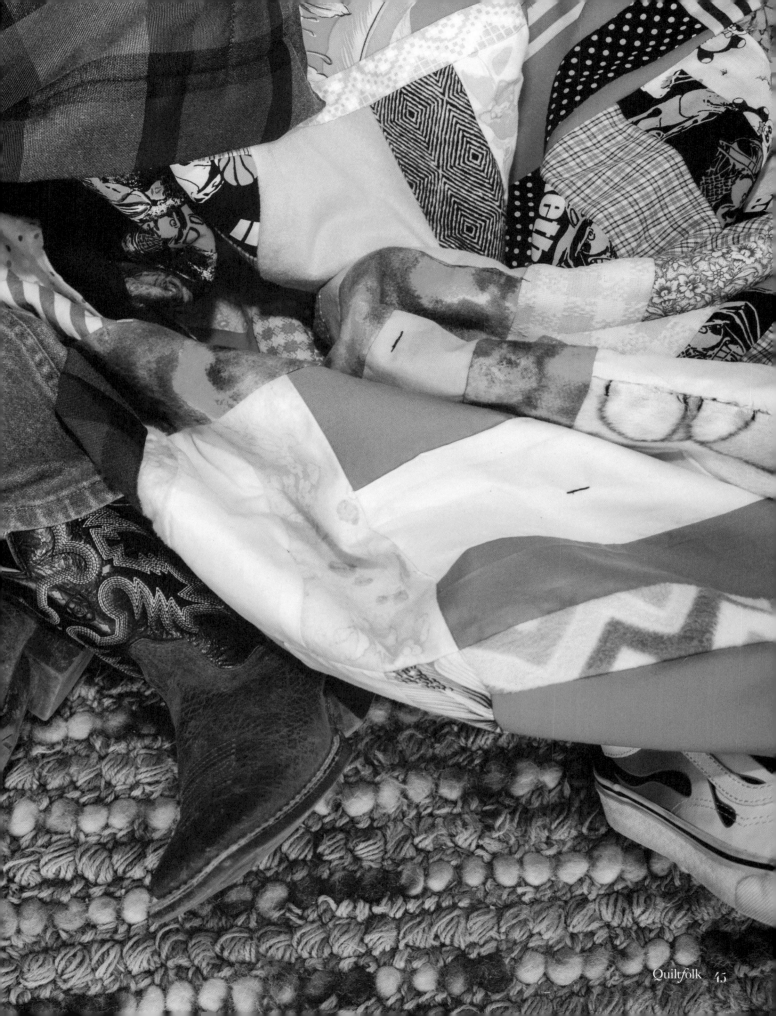

TOP: The young women of Owyhee High, from left: Lilli, Daeja, Alyna, MiKayla, Kayla, Jenna, Brianna, MaKinzie, and Shaquala.
BOTTOM: A classroom quilt, made with love.

The young men of Owyhee, from left: Julian, Rigo, Klay, Sequoia, Gage, and Devin.

Cady says eventually she would like to make her own clothes, and Ms. Reed is eager to teach garment sewing. Ribbon skirts and shirts are traditional garments of the Shoshone-Paiute tribe, and her students have expressed an interest in learning to make heritage clothing.

"Sometimes we have an Indigenous Day here at the school and people wear the ribbon skirts and ribbon shirts to show off," Johnson said with a roll of the eyes. But Johnson said he'd be interested in learning how to make the traditional garments. "If we learned how, I would try it," he said. "That's kind of our tradition, and I could pass it down to my kids

and keep it going. It'd be nice."

Cady sees the potential quilts have to do the same thing.

"With quilts, you can look at other patterns that your ancestors did and then take the patterns and use them," she said. "I think it'd be really cool to try that."

Like Cady, most of the kids say they enjoy sewing and will continue if they get the chance. A proud Ms. Reed hopes what her students learn in home economics class will stay with them just as her own home ec class has stayed with her after all this time.

STRING BLOCK TUTORIAL

String blocks are fun and great scrap-busters.
Follow these steps to make your own.

MATERIALS

☐ Scraps of quilting cotton

☐ Foundation paper
(any lightweight paper such as newsprint will do)

☐ Sewing machine, threaded

☐ Scissors

☐ Pins (optional)

METHOD

1. Cut foundation paper into squares of desired finished size plus seam allowances.

2. Place one strip of fabric face up along the bottom edge of paper square, making sure the strip completely covers the paper.

3. Place a second strip of fabric *face down* on top of the first strip; make sure to align the raw edges that are closer to the center of the square. If desired, loosely pin fabric to paper to temporarily secure.

4. Shorten the sewing machine's stitch length to 1.4 or 1.8. Sew the strips together with a ¼" seam along the aligned edges. Press the second strip open.

5. Continue stitching and flipping strips until paper square is covered.

6. Trim edges flush with paper square; tear off foundation paper.

Special thanks to Julian for sharing his process.

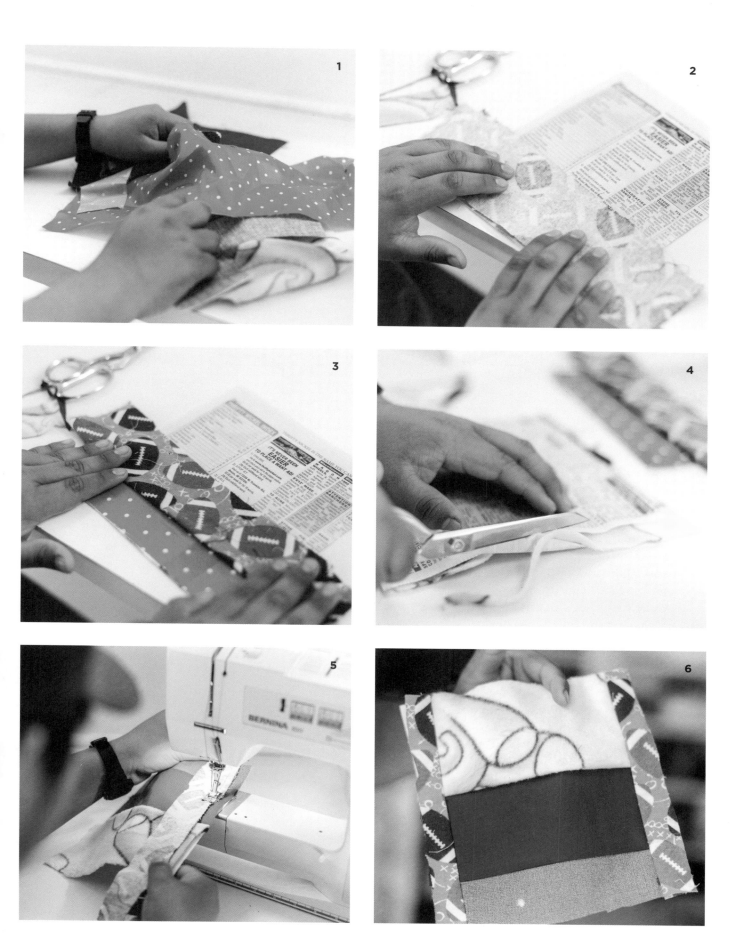

BY **Meg Cox**

Crimson Rose
ETERNAL FLAME

Crimson Rose's sewing machine sits under a dust cover she made from fabric with a flame motif. As she shows a blue-and-white quilt she made a few years ago, a tattoo of flames can be seen snaking up her left wrist. This theme of fire is appropriate: Crimson Rose is known to tens of thousands in the Burning Man community as "The Fire Goddess."

Fire is the central theme of Burning Man, an annual event that draws 75,000-plus people to Nevada's harsh, uninhabited Black Rock Desert the week before Labor Day. What started out more than 30 years ago as a small, counterculture bacchanal on a San Francisco beach has evolved into a communal, art-focused event that turns the grounds, called "the playa," into a vibrant, temporary city. Several hundred large sculptures are built on the playa each year, and participants are invited to climb, swing, and play on the art. The storied highlight of the week takes place on Saturday night, when a 40-foot-tall stylized neon stick figure of a man is burned in a raucous (but uplifting) ceremony.

The Nevada artist and occasional "Fire Goddess" Crimson Rose in her studio.

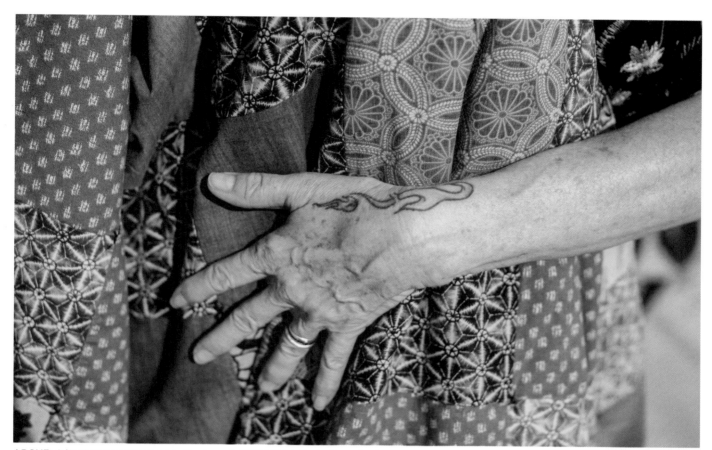

ABOVE: A hot tattoo and a cool quilt mix well. OPPOSITE: Under Nevada skies, artistic souls like Rose are free to pursue art and community.

Rose, whose birth name is known only to a few, was instrumental in coaxing the focus of Burning Man toward art. Looking at her, it's clear she's an artistic soul. The first striking thing about Rose is the thick, straight white hair that cascades past her shoulders (it started turning white in high school, she said). Dressed in all black except for the embroidered purple flowers on her flowing blouse, Rose's "vibe" is a potent cross between Earth goddess and rock star. She owns any space she inhabits, still moving with the grace of the former professional dancer she is. But her charisma is paired with genuine warmth: Rose immediately started making coffee for the *Quiltfolk* crew as we entered her kitchen.

Quilts have been in Rose's life since childhood and she keeps several special quilts from that time. She deeply treasures an inherited Lone Star quilt made by her grandmother, an important figure in

her life. "I would stay at my maternal grandmother's place, where they had every kind of fruit tree, and rabbits and chickens," Rose said. "I remember sleeping under this quilt … Just touching it releases beautiful memories to me."

Rose's grandmother didn't teach her to quilt, but she and Rose's mother raised her to knit, sew, and embroider to conserve and appreciate textile beauty, and to simply enjoy artistic play. Knitting has been a constant for Rose most of her life; dyeing fabric is a more recent passion. It wasn't until a few years ago that she finally tried patchwork.

"I'm just not one for throwing stuff out if it's in good shape," she said, holding up a thick, curved-edge, oversized bed quilt. "This is a perfect example. I had this old, enormous comforter that was falling apart and I had a pile of these blue patterned fabric squares, so I stitched a patchwork cover on my Singer."

ABOVE: Beyond the quilt, an Airstream camper awaits adventure. OPPOSITE: Detail, signature quilt made by Rose's grandmother, Mabel Viola Meador (ca. 1940); Cracker Jack blocks bear the names of relatives as well as members of Meador's quilting group.

MRS CHAPMAN

I Della Brown

Rose and her partner, artist Will Roger.

In Gerlach, a tiny town near the open landscape where Burning Man occurs, Rose uses the "heavy duty" Singer sewing machine she's had for several years. When she and partner Will Roger are in their Oakland residence (the home office is closer to Burning Man's San Francisco roots), she sews on a Bernina with computerized embroidery capability.

Here in the desert, in her light-filled art studio, Rose surrounds herself with objects she loves to see and touch — and that second aspect is crucial. Her instinct, she says, has always been to have a tactile experience with art and craft.

"I'm an art toucher," Rose said. "A couple years ago, I was in a Seattle museum and was startled by this voice over the loudspeaker saying, 'Don't touch the art!' I thought at the time, 'Oh, God, now I'm gonna get arrested!' When I go into a fabric store, it's the same thing: I'm going to touch everything — although [those shops] are fine with touching."

That attitude about having a direct experience of art is integral to the Burning Man experience, where there are no velvet ropes or informational plaques near the artworks displayed. "We realized if someone wasn't interacting with it, the art wasn't complete," Rose said, "it was just a *thing*, very static. It is a person's participation that makes Burning Man. Otherwise it would just be a camping trip in the desert where we burn a 40-foot man."

CLOCKWISE FROM UPPER LEFT: Shibori work in the studio; wind chimes sway in the desert breeze; Rose and Roger built the Casa El Rancho Labyrinth in 2015 and walk it daily, rain or shine.

ABOVE: One of four *OpaLights* statues on the property; the "robots" were designed and built for Burning Man 2018 by California artist Opa, then gifted to Rose and Roger. **OPPOSITE:** In the studio, an artist's curios and mementos.

ABOVE: Detail, our Issue 15 "cover girl" quilt, a gift to Rose from Grandmother Meador. OPPOSITE: When she saw her quilt hanging on the door to her partner's Cowboy Zen Garden, Rose said, "My grandmother's spirit is here."

Because of occasional dust storms and winds across the playa that can whip up to 60 miles an hour, quilts don't show up too often at Burning Man. But in 2019, an intrepid California quilter named Michelle Tarantino managed *Transition in Comfort*, a piece that consisted of three quilts in a row telling the story of her depression. The "batting" inside each was the rugged quilted blankets movers use, and Tarantino used heavy duty wire to hold them in place. She went for it, she said, because the atmosphere at Burning Man "is the most accepting place I've ever been. What did I have to lose?"

Tarantino's words are music to Rose's ears, and she was thrilled to see quilts hold their own at Burning Man.

For Crimson Rose, interactive art and ritual are the twin pillars that make Burning Man remarkable. When she first attended the event in 1991, she was an experienced "fire dancer," a performance practice she picked up during her years in San Francisco. She earned the nickname "Fire Goddess" because she has helped create and nurture various fire ceremonies that happen yearly on the playa, starting with the first Monday of the event, when she uses a magnifying glass to light a fire inside a filigree-topped cauldron called El Diabla.

This summer, Rose won't be out on the playa lighting the ritual fire as thousands watch: In April, Burning Man was cancelled due to the coronavirus pandemic. Crimson Rose intends to light El Diabla next year. Until then, she'll tend to her own artistic fire, a flame that refuses to be extinguished.

GO WEST

An Eclectic Adventure

GO WEST

YOU'LL FIND BOTH SILVER AND GOLD in the part of Nevada tucked inside the elbow of California, east of Lake Tahoe and north of the Sierra Nevada mountains.

In the legendary silver mining town of Virginia City, you can follow a wooden boardwalk into establishments like the Bucket of Blood Saloon, established in 1876. An open call on social media brought local quilters to that picturesque town for the first-ever *Quiltfolk* show-and-tell.

A different scene meets you just a few dozen miles away in Reno. Nearly a century ago, Nevada passed statewide laws that made divorce quick and gambling legal; Reno was early in making itself *the* hip place to do both. In 1929, Reno nicknamed itself "The Biggest Little City in the World," and its casinos and glitzy dance shows attracted millions. Over time, however, Las Vegas attracted more star power. Today, the storied city of Reno, dotted with tattoo parlors and high-rise casinos, celebrates both its glamour and its grit.

Reno's blend of low taxes and business incentives have ushered in something of a renaissance, creating a massive migration from California, especially Silicon Valley. Tesla, Amazon, and other big companies are developing the area, and artists are flooding in too, with funky shops and murals flowering all over downtown.

It was in this part of Nevada that we found gold in Karen Burns's trove of showgirl costumes, explored Christa Watson's "Quilt House," and discovered much more. Follow us as we part the beaded curtain to look at another side of Nevada.

Faithful Friends

BY **Kestrel Michaud**

In the heart of Reno's sprawling Renown Regional Medical Center, on the back wall of a tranquil chapel, hangs a quilt of many colors. The quilt is beautiful, but what it stands for approaches miraculous.

The quilt, titled *Coming Together,* was created and donated by members of the Nevada Clergy Association, which later became the Nevada Interfaith Association (NIA). The NIA is a multi-faith network that aims to increase mutual understanding and respect among religious and spiritual people in Nevada.

Patricia Meidell, an NIA member and a public affairs director for the Church of Jesus Christ of Latter-day Saints, attended an interfaith luncheon in 2014. When the talk turned to the 150th year of Nevada's statehood, Meidell had an idea for a sesquicentennial quilt.

Meidell knew that a quilt is a universal object, that people of all walks of life and religious traditions make quilts. Meidell's own church has a long history of quilting; Mormon missionary groups that settled in the West in the 1800s sometimes offered quiltmaking lessons to the indigenous peoples they met in hopes they'd come to church. Looking around the room, Meidell thought about all of the different faith stories represented there that day. Meidell, though not a quiltmaker herself but someone with huge admiration for quilts and the people who make them, thought to herself, "Hmm ... I wonder if anybody here makes quilts."

Meidell asked around and quickly discovered that in fact many NIA members were quiltmakers. The idea of a group quilt that would recognize religious diversity as part of Nevada's sesquicentennial celebration was on its way.

With this project, "I thought we could do two things," said Meidell. "We could pull this together — or stitch *us* together, as the case may be — to do something as an outward display of our unity." Making a quilt would also give the NIA the ability "to demonstrate who we are in northern Nevada."

Inside the Estelle J. Kelsey Interfaith Sanctuary, six quiltmakers gather for a portrait. Back row, L-R: Patricia Meidell, Nahla Kadry, Radjeka Savoy; front row, L-R: Ellyn Darrah, Shelly Fisher, Noriko Roy, and Jackie Manley.

ABOVE: A dove with an olive branch on the Trinity Episcopal Church block. **OPPOSITE:** Blue sashing unites the participants' message while giving each block space to be counted.

> *"If we look for what we have in common instead of hating the differences,*
> *we stand a much better chance of living in harmony."*
>
> — ELLYN DARRAH

Coming Together is made up of 15 distinct blocks separated by blue sashing. The center block celebrates Nevada — state pride being something all the quiltmakers have in common. The 14 blocks surrounding the center block represent the respective faith tradition of each participant.

Noriko Roy's yellow and red block in the lower left shows Om, one of the most important spiritual symbols in Hinduism. Jackie Manley was inspired by a watercolor painting of the original meeting place of the First Congregational Church of Reno back in 1871, so she recreated the painting on her block. Some of the other blocks in the quilt represent the Bahá'í Faith, Judaism, Islam, Buddhism, and even the non-organized faith group Witches and Heathens, a network of practitioners who seek harmony with nature.

The 14 makers of the blocks indeed created a patchwork representation of inherent bonds shared between their religious communities. "The quilt is a beautiful symbol of that inclusiveness and unity that is a model for our community at large," said Rev. Shelley Fisher of the Reno Buddhist Center.

As anyone who has worked on a group or "bee" quilt can attest, there were "make it work" moments. Ellyn Darrah, a Vietnam veteran and quilter who made the Children of the Temple Earth block, said things got "a little lopsided. I had it pinned, but somebody *un*pinned it when they were putting it all together." She laughed. "It got tipped, but you know what? That's okay."

Rev. Fisher agreed: "It's not perfect. *We're* not perfect."

Those involved in the NIA quilt project were already interacting and cooperating with each other before the idea for this quilt was born, but the *Coming Together* quilt is visual proof that a diverse assemblage of people can get along despite their adherence to different religions.

"If we look for what we have in common instead of hating the differences," said Darrah, "we stand a much better chance of living in harmony." ◯

From upper left, reading left to right, *Coming Together* includes blocks representing Trinity Episcopal Church; International Community of Christ; the Bahá'í Faith; Lutheran congregations; Our Lady of the Snows, Diocese of Reno; Church of Jesus Christ of Latter-day Saints; Temple Sinai; Temple Beth Or; the Hindu community; Children of Temple Earth; Unitarian Universalist Fellowship of Northern Nevada; the Buddhist community; the Northern Nevada Muslim community; and First Congregational Church.

BY **Meg Cox**

Karen Burns

HELLO, QUILTS!

In black slacks and a pinstripe jacket, a double strand of pearls looped around her neck, Karen Burns led the *Quiltfolk* team through a packed but well-organized warehouse. Here is where Burns keeps her vintage costumes, and where she brought a few special quilts for a VIP show-and-tell.

First, she held up a showgirl headdress decorated with a dozen floaty ostrich boas and 25 pheasant feathers. The feathers, dyed black, bristled upward from the radiating spikes of the sparkly crown, studded with 625 Swarovski crystals and some 75 small mirrors, all sewn on by hand. Burns held the piece upside down so she could point out an intricate criss-cross pattern of taupe-colored stitches inside the dome.

The glamorous Karen Burns safeguards showgirl history
and a few special quilts in Reno.

ABOVE: Detail, a patchwork bedspread Burns made in 1972 out of scraps of homemade dresses. OPPOSITE: Burns's mission in life is to keep alive the fascinating history of stage show costumes.

"People don't realize that these costumes were designed by people with haute couture backgrounds," said Burns. "The workmanship was astounding."

Back in the day, when Reno was cooler than Vegas and showgirl shoes were made by Parisian artisans, glamorous stage shows were not just supple girls doing high kicks wearing maximum bling; they were also a "show" of extreme craftsmanship with needle and thread.

Burns shared with us that her appreciation of cloth and needle skills started long ago. Navigating through racks of sparkly clothes and boxes piled high with wigs, she came to the table where she had laid out a quilt. Made when she was in high school, the simple blocks were composed of scraps

of dresses she had sewn for herself. As she touched the different squares, she reminisced about their origin outfits.

In 1981, she hung up her feather boas and began using her show biz know-how to produce hundreds of corporate, casino, and convention shows about the golden showgirl era. Mostly she had to design and create costumes for herself and dancers she hired for these events, scrounging around thrift stores and repurposing garments into something with convincing razzle-dazzle. It helped to have had so much experience making her own garments, including a favorite: a long patchwork skirt she made in high school. "It was the hippie era and homemade was cool then," she recalled.

ABOVE: A patchwork clown costume designed by Pete Menefee for the 1970s show *Hello Hollywood, Hello*. **OPPOSITE:** Detail of a bodysuit covered with sequins and Swarovski rhinestones.

ABOVE, L-R: A very 1970s puffy patchwork pillow; Burns with a quilt from husband Ted's side of the family, made by his great aunt Esther, ca. 1930s. **OPPOSITE:** Burns made this apron for her mother for Christmas around 1976; four other female family members got aprons, too.

Money was tight in her family. Burns comes from a long line of frugal crafters, and grew up using her sewing skills to turn out gifts for special occasions: handmade aprons, pillows, and quilts for babies and brides. She didn't know back then she would one day be plying a needle to maintain a vast collection of showgirl finery.

Karen Burns is uniquely qualified to preserve and share this history: She lived it. As a young woman, Burns took ballet lessons to improve as a competitive freestyle skier. By the time she got to college, her dance skills were strong enough to land her a summer gig at a nightclub. She would eventually spend nearly two years as a chorus dancer in the extravagant stage show *Hello Hollywood, Hello: A Tribute to the Magic World of*

Movies at the MGM Grand Hotel in Reno.

Burns never forgot those exquisite costumes from her MGM years, and when the famous *Hello Hollywood, Hello* show finally closed in 1989 after 11 years, she bought more than 1,200 costumes, becoming an unorthodox curator and caretaker of a vivid chapter in entertainment history.

All those years of trying to replicate the real thing taught her to truly appreciate the MGM costumes for the handcrafted treasures they are: As one of 142 performers, changing costumes eight to 10 times in a single performance, Burns knows that it took a wardrobe staff of 54 people, more than twice the size of the show's orchestra, to keep all those clothes clean and repaired.

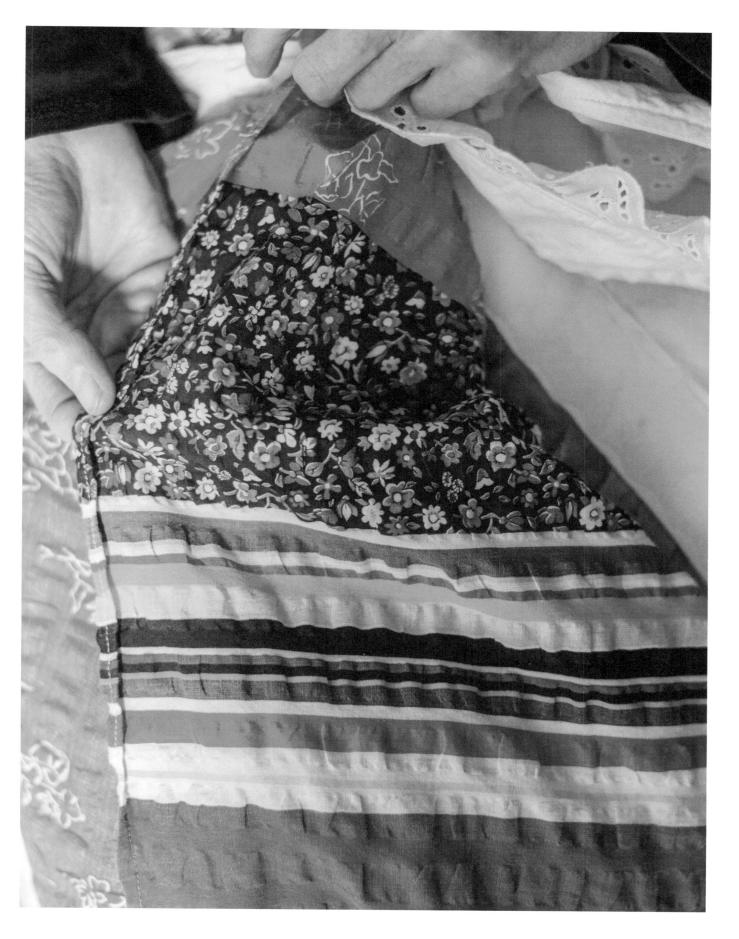

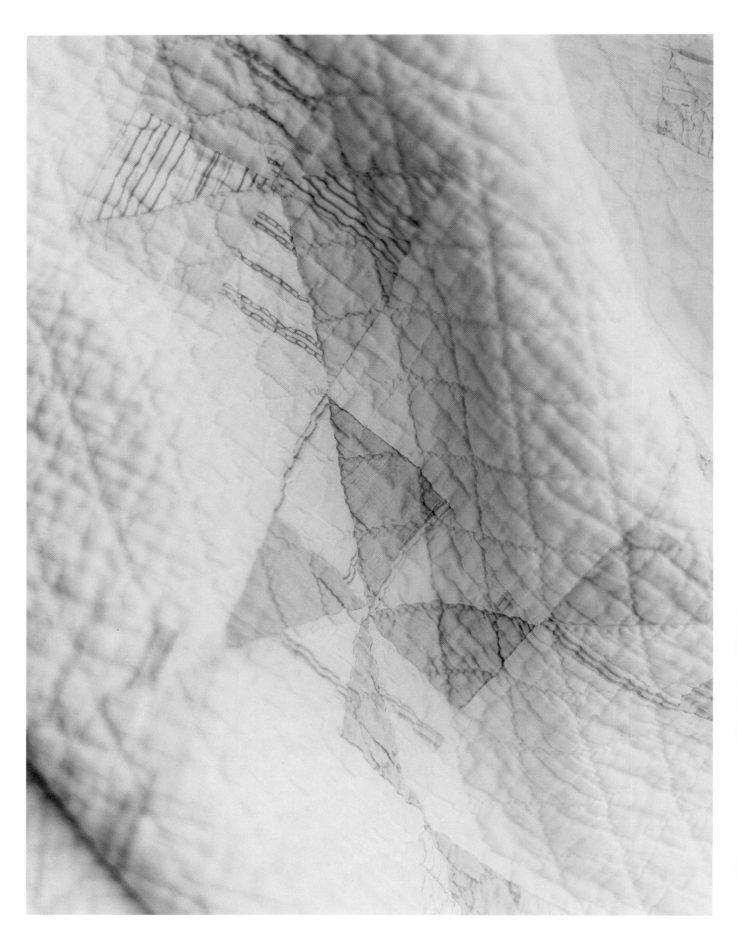

ABOVE: A quilter-showgirl in her element. OPPOSITE: A handwritten note pinned to the back of this quilt (ca. 1930s) from Ted's family reads: "Grandpa Mac's mother made this out of his shirts."

Now, she is the one who dips into buckets of tubular bugle beads to replace those that fall off.

For Burns, her trove of costumes is her livelihood, but she surrounds herself with other textiles for the joy of it, including knit and crochet items from her family and dozens of quilts from her husband's family. She brings out several favorites, including a bed-sized quilt that modern quilters would swoon over: a mostly white background punctuated by delicate pinwheel squares in faded blues, grays, and reds. "This was made by [my husband] Ted's great-grandmother out of his grandfather's shirts, about a century ago," Burns said, with obvious affection.

These days, few genuine showgirls are left. Entertainment trends have shifted, and not just in Reno. Celebrity singers such as Celine Dion and shows like Cirque du Soleil now dominate Nevada's high-roller towns. Regardless, Burns is intent on keeping the stitches and stories intact.

"I still don't know exactly how I wound up here," Burns said with her earthy laugh, "but I feel that costumes are art and they tell history. Just like there is a history of each one of my quilts, these costumes have stories. The stories, the stories!"

BY **Kestrel Michaud**

OPEN BOOKS
RENO'S LIBRARY QUILT

A visit to the Downtown Reno Library is a refreshing experience. Outside, the streets are hot, dusty, and dry (the metropolitan city is in the middle of a desert, after all) but inside the library, it's peaceful and quiet, and subtropical life is thriving.

Visitors who open the tinted glass doors and step inside are greeted by trees — yes, actual trees — growing up from the first floor. Yard after yard of pothos vines and spider plants tumble down from the high ceiling above. Visible through the greenery is a spiral staircase connecting four stories of library shelves positively packed with books.

And tucked into a nook near the stairs, hidden among the plants and pages of this unique library, are books of another kind. In a spot almost invisible from the entrance hangs a little quilt. Like the shelves surrounding it, this quilt is full of books: 36 of them to be exact, each partially open, each cover cut from a different cloth. The quilt was made by members of the Truckee Meadows Quilters and donated to the library in 1993. Each of those who created a book block put their name on the spine.

The fabrics chosen for the book covers reflect the diversity and extremes of the landscape and climate outside. Small calico prints, bold florals, sun-bleached pastels, and deep indigos and burgundies seem to represent some of the many moods of Nevada's terrain. This colorful quilt speaks volumes about the creative inspiration behind it. It's a patchwork jewel in the center of Reno's not-so-secret literary garden. *QF*

There's a quilt to be found in the splendor of Reno's downtown library.

FROM LEFT: Books on the "shelves" in the quilt; the trees and plants provide a peaceful environment for readers; the library quilt tells a story of Reno quiltmakers.

RENO NEVADA

1993

BY **Kestrel Michaud**

Show-and-Tell
NEVADA STYLE

A former mining boomtown sits atop a windswept mountain in western Nevada. In the 19th century, Virginia City was bustling with activity. The mines closed long ago, but the city continues to thrive. Though its population hovers around just 1,000 people, Virginia City has retained its Wild West character and flair with a main street full of saloons, general stores, and wooden walkways.

It was this historic town that was chosen as the backdrop for a monumental event: the first-ever, official, large-scale *Quiltfolk* show-and-tell. Several weeks before the big day, *Quiltfolk* invited any interested Nevada quilter or quilt enthusiast to bring a quilt to Virginia City at the appointed time. They could share quilt stories, meet locals from their own quilting community, and put on display what makes Nevada quilters so awesome.

Attending this event was not for the faint of heart, it turned out. There was no denying it: It was cold. It was windy. Before the day was done, it was ... snowing. Not an ideal forecast for an outdoor show-and-tell; regardless, 44 dedicated Nevada ladies (plus a handful of their husbands) braved the elements.

On facing page, clockwise from upper left: Arriving in Virginia City; Lynn Roldao keeps warm with a quilt; the streets of a picturesque, historic town; show-and-teller Sheri Smith brought her quilt — and her mittens.

Linda de Smet Colin pieced *Soiled Doves In The Window* with fabric from a 2012 guild challenge; she said the floral print reminded her of wallpaper in an old-time Nevada brothel.

Quiltfolk fans who came to Virginia City weren't going to let a little spring breeze keep them from meeting fellow quiltmakers.

CLOCKWISE FROM TOP: A few of Nevada's finest; Nancy Ward is all smiles; Antoinette Davis brought a quilt and a coat. **OPPOSITE:** Laurie Lile (center) holds a quilted picture of Nevada. At left, Randi King and Jennifer Beadman; at right, Sheila Walker's dog Penney in patchwork.

Lynsey Hatfield shows off a modern-style mini-quilt as a Christmas tree skirt-wearing Jennifer Beadman admires her work.

Kathryn Emanuel brought a quilt she made with a Deb Strain panel and fabric purchased while on a trip with quilting friends to Liberty, Missouri.

CLOCKWISE FROM TOP: Friends Lisa Snavely (left) and Millie Szerman took inspiration from the many bears they see in their part of Nevada; the tip-top of the old schoolhouse; Sherri Smith looks on. OPPOSITE: A boisterous show-and-tell, Nevada style.

A gathering of show-and-tellers pose for a group picture at a neighborhood gazebo.

The diverse group, sharing the personal stories behind an eclectic collection of quilts, made for a touching sight. Novices and veterans, traditionalists and art quilters alike came together in Virginia City that day. The quilts they brought with them ran the gamut from challenge quilts and award-winners to rediscovered family heirlooms. Yet the commonality between each and every one was how meaningful the quilt was to its creator. All these quilts were beloved.

Every participant we spoke with proved what we already suspected: Nevada quilters are passionate and enthusiastic, whatever the weather.

Sarah Joe McKee brought a quilt that she said was "the result of a very long endeavor" to collect as much of Cotton+Steel's original fabric line as possible. She kept collecting until she found a pattern she liked, which she then adapted. McKee said that she gives away many of her quilts, "but this is one I've held onto for myself."

When asked why she chose to bring this particular quilt to the show-and-tell, the answer was simple: "The colors make me happy."

Diana Pargeon brought a quilt sewn by her great-great-grandmother in 1880. The quilt had been locked away in a closet for years. "My aunt was going to [give it] to a museum," Pargeon said. "But I said, 'No, it's going in my sewing room.'"

Just off Virginia City's main drag, a breakout group of quiltmakers share quilts (and warmth).

Then there were the two ladies who came to Virginia City together and described themselves as "a packaged deal."

"We started quilting back in 2000," said Linda Camlin, "though I've been a wannabe quilter for —"

"Forever," Randy King interjected.

"Much longer than that," said Camlin, who said she began collecting how-to books and supplies in the 1970s because, as she put it, "I was getting ready!"

"We've both sewn for most of our lives," King said, "and we're two fairly intelligent women, so [we thought] surely we could quilt."

"Yeah, and then it took us *hours* to make a block," Camlin said, laughing.

King and Camlin came to the event as old friends, but new friendships were forged that day too.

"I learned how to sew when I was young," said Lynsey Hatfield, the youngest attendee that day. "A couple of years ago I just decided I wanted to make a quilt. I bought a foundation-piecing pattern and just jumped in. That was my first one and I've never looked back."

She'll soon be looking forward: "This is the first community event I've ever been to," said Hatfield. "Two of the ladies [here] have already invited me to [join] the Modern Quilt Guild."

That kind of connection was just what we hoped would happen at a *Quiltfolk* "all-state" show-and-tell. 𝒬𝒻

Travels with Rosie

At the first-ever Quiltfolk *show-and-tell in Virginia City, one sunny quilt caught our eye. Here, Nevada quiltmaker Lynsey Hatfield shares the story behind a quilt she hopes will always be in bloom.*

As my quiltmaking practice has grown, I've begun to notice a drive to incorporate more handwork in my quilts. I truly love the act of stitching with my hands, enjoying the rhythm of my needle. Hand stitching (whether I'm piecing, quilting, embroidering, or doing appliqué), offers me control over placement, precision, and portability.

This desire for controlled flexibility has led me to hexagonal Mosaic patchwork, commonly referred to as English Paper Piecing. Making "hexies" is a methodical process: You wrap each hexagon paper with fabric, align every edge, then secure each corner to the next.

This special quilt, which I'm calling *Rosie's Quilt,* was inspired by the traditional Grandmother's Flower Garden pattern. I enjoy having a general guide to follow when making quilts, but I gravitate toward designs that offer flexibility. A design that begins with a hexie flower as a base is a great example: You can begin with a single flower and grow a quilt around it.

Rosie's Quilt is for my goddaughter, a little girl who radiates pure joy for life and an untarnished curiosity for the world. I wanted to create a quilt Rosie would not only enjoy looking at, but one that she could carry with her through life. That meant I needed to design something that would feel modern but still traditional enough to remain appealing as she grows and learns about herself and the things that bring her joy.

My hope is that this quilt will give my exuberant goddaughter comfort while encouraging a curiosity for exploration, and this led me to an overarching travel theme.

The central print I chose to use for the quilt ("Amalfi Explorer" by Cotton+Steel) showcases a handful of distant locations that remind me of the wealth of variety our world offers. These motifs, which I placed in the center of each hexie, are intended to motivate Rosie to travel and learn about other people and cultures.

For the petals, I chose to complement the fussy-cut centers with colorful, nature-inspired prints. Then, starting with the same hexagon papers I used for he flowers — this time cutting them into diamonds and triangles — I designed gem-like shapes to fill the spaces around the flowers in the "garden." When these pieces were ready, I sat on the floor, arranging them over and over until I had a design I felt was worthy of the completed flowers.

I hope that the careful design I've created will inspire my goddaughter to pour herself into her own passions. I also hope Rosie's very own quilt will help hold a place for me in her mind through the years when the miles separate us. Even now, Rosie and I live on opposite sides of the country; visits are rare and always too short.

I look forward to seeing this quilt age with every reunion. I suspect I'll continue to enjoy the rhythm of handwork, so I will continue to bring a needle and thread in my carryon whenever I go to visit my goddaughter, eager with anticipation of frayed seams and other signs that the gifted quilt has been loved. Starting now, I hope Rosie will grow to see my love for her in every mended tear, patched stain, and that distinctive crinkle that emerges from every hand-placed stitch.

LAS VEGAS
Viva Las Quilters

LAS VEGAS

CASINOS! SHOWGIRLS! FRANK SINATRA! And who could forget that famously sly slogan: "What happens in Vegas, stays in Vegas."

It's natural to think of Las Vegas in such flashy terms (there's a reason the place's nickname is "Sin City"). But for the 3 million year-round residents — the people who actually do stay in Vegas — the Strip is just one point of pride. Galleries and performance spaces are blooming in an energized arts district; food-lovers flock to the city for world-class cuisine; and family-friendly parks and museums are a world away from a crowded blackjack table.

Every local we met was eager to talk about the natural beauty of the southernmost tip of Nevada. Today, Vegas is known for its dry, arid climate, but when Spanish explorers established the area in 1829, they actually stopped for water: Artesian springs once bubbled here, prompting the explorers to give the city its name, which translates to "the meadows." If you're seeking a Las Vegas experience more akin to the explorers', visit in the winter months when mild temperatures encourage outdoor activities like hiking, rock climbing, and skydiving. And don't forget: The Grand Canyon is just a five-hour drive from "Glitter Gulch."

We're sure you'll enjoy quilt stories from the real Las Vegas. You'll visit a quilter who works (a lot!) from home, get to know a special guild, and meet some next-generation shop owners in the city.

Welcome to Fabulous Las Vegas!

BY **Riane Menardi Morrison**

Full House

A TALE OF TWO SHOPS

———————

A family that quilts together stays together. If that's true, then Nevada may be the best place in the country to open a family-run quilt shop.

The Las Vegas quilt shop scene is dominated by two quilting powerhouses, both of them family affairs. A pair of glamorous sisters serve the southeastern metro area; three good-natured brothers run the northwest side. All five entrepreneurs are born-and-bred Las Vegans, proud to take the reins of their families' shops.

Passionate and dedicated, the ladies of Quiltique (top) and the guys at Sew Yeah Quilting are Vegas's next-generation shop owners.

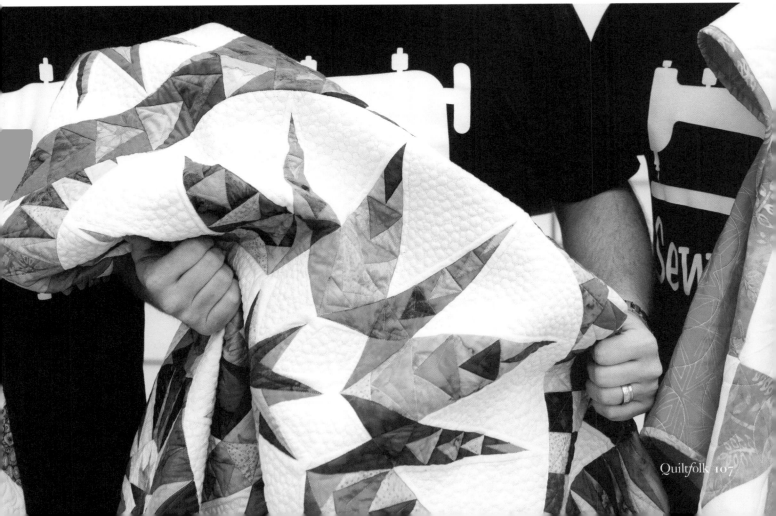

Jennifer Albaugh and Kara Tibesar
QUILTIQUE'S GLAMOUR GIRLS

In January of 2003, the Tibesar family — Bob, Jan, and daughters Kara Tibesar and Jennifer Albaugh — decided to open a quilt shop in Henderson. Within just four months, they turned a family's idea into a family business, relying on each other's unique skills to make it happen.

As a quilter with a background in accounting, Jan Tibesar, responsible for the idea in the first place, brought her finance skills to the table. Husband Bob, an architect and engineer, could design the store's layout and run the machine department. Jennifer, an alumna of New York's esteemed Fashion Institute of Technology (FIT), had studied marketing and merchandise management. And Kara, the artist in the family, would lend her discerning eye to the shop's fabric and products and could also manage customer service. It was a dream team, and the Tibesar family opened the doors to Quiltique in April 2003.

Now in its 17th year of business, Quiltique is a quilt shop with a high profile in Las Vegas and beyond. .

"One of the biggest compliments we get is when customers come in and say, 'I live in Canada, and my friend said if you're going to Vegas, you have to go to this shop,'" Kara Tibesar said. "When we hear that, we love it. People coming from all over to see us is really cool."

Tibesar and Albaugh are born and raised Las Vegans ("a rare breed" as they say). They love their community of locals as well as the visitors who come to their city to have a good time.

"Sometimes they say, 'I'm not gambling. I saved my money for your store, for fabric,'" Albaugh said with a smile.

"Or they did win at gambling and then they come here!" Tibesar said. "It's awesome."

No matter where their customers come from, or for what reason, the sisters are passionate about building community and creating an inspiring place for quilters to shop for fabric, take classes, and get help with projects.

Said Albaugh: "It's hard in a big city to have a small-community feel, but with our great customers and just quilting in general, it brings so much. We get this hometown feeling because of our quilting community."

"I meet someone every day from some other part of the world, and we all have quilting in common," Tibesar said. In this way, everyone who comes into the shop might as well be family.

Through it all, the Tibesar family supports their customers, just like they support each other. "There's not a day I can remember where I'm not excited to go to work," Tibesar said.

"It's just nice that we are a family business and we enjoy what we do after all this time," Albaugh said. "After 17 years, I still like to come here."

Sisters Kara Tibesar (left) and Jennifer Albaugh bring energy and glamour to their family's business, in operation since 2003.
NEXT PAGE: Keeping warm with quilts made by Mom. Around Tibesar, *Half Moon Quilt* (2017); around Albaugh, *Jewel Squares* (1998). Both patterns by Kaffe Fassett.

The Tippetts Brothers
SEW YEAH QUILTING

Sew Yeah Quilting began at the dinner table, as the Tippetts family enjoyed a family meal.

"My mom came home and said, 'You know what, I've been thinking we should open up a quilt shop,'" said Brody Tippetts, the middle of three brothers and co-owner of Sew Yeah. Wild ideas were common in the Tippetts household; at one point, someone had suggested the family open a salmon hatchery in Alaska, for example. So, as for becoming quilt shop owners, Brody said, "everyone just kind of laughed — we didn't think much of it."

But this idea actually took hold. At the time, Brody was in school studying to be a paramedic. His older brother, Zach, had just finished his master's degree in social work, and Teancum was involved with a mission trip in South America. But the brothers had to admit the sewing industry intrigued them. At home together again in Las Vegas, they set to work learning how to run a quilt shop.

When they opened their doors, Sew Yeah only carried bolts of fabric, so when a customer asked for fat quarters, they didn't exactly know what those were. Realizing there was a lot they didn't know about running a quilt-related business, they went where they knew they could find answers: International Quilt Market, he twice-annual show that has served as the heartbeat of the commercial quilt world for more than four decades.

"We got a crash course in three days," said Brody. "We had to learn everything: what size of rotary cutter is best, what are the best brands of scissors, what's the best sewing machine … Our training was Quilt Market."

Today, the brothers are experts at running their shop — and they even sample their product.

"We used to be 'guys that owned a quilt shop,' and it wasn't like we were super big quilters," Brody said. "But then it was like, if we're going to do this, we really need to know what we're doing."

So the "guys" learned to quilt. Today, their YouTube channel has over 34,000 subscribers who tune in to see the three quilting Tippetts execute dozens of quilting tutorials.

Sew Yeah is first and foremost a business, but the Tippetts love what they do, especially because it means working with family. They say their mom is still involved, but — aside from giving the brothers a few motherly suggestions here and there — she's mostly a customer. Even their two younger sisters, who are 18 and 19, work at the shop.

When the Tippetts brothers were asked if they always knew they wanted to be partners, the answer was a resounding yes. Said Zach, "We grew up working together, so [the shop] was the natural progression of what was already going. We're really a tight-knit family."

From left, Brody, Zach, and Teancum Tippetts know that family matters.

Triple trouble: Zach holds a Delectable Mountain quilt designed by Brody; Brody holds *Dream Flight* quilt (pattern by Jacqueline De Jonge); Teancum holds a quilt he designed himself, *Modern Bear Paw Star Quilt*. **OPPOSITE:** Vintage Vegas on display at the "Neon Boneyard."

BY **Mary Fons**

Colleen Hall-Patton
MATERIAL GIRL

———————

If a person is a dedicated quiltmaker, she's kind of a scholar, too.

Consider how she can ruminate for days, even months, on her next project. She is able to hold opposing ideas in her mind as she considers design options. She may study the stitches on a prize-winning quilt. When she repeatedly reviews a particularly tough pattern at her sewing table, that's homework.

But every once in a while, a quiltmaker desires to study quilts *as a topic*, to pursue quilt scholarship in the formal sense. (This is often at the expense of her quilt projects, but that's another story.) This quilt scholar, be she amateur or professional, desires to examine the space quilts occupy in society, history, or other contexts that interest her.

Quilts definitely interest author, professor, and sociologist Colleen Hall-Patton. This interest has spanned decades and she's a triple-threat: a scholar, a casual collector, and a real-life quiltmaker. With that much quilt scholarship, it's a wonder Hall-Patton has mental space to be interested in anything else.

Colleen Hall-Patton holds a LeMoyne Star quilt from 1860. "More than 150 years later," she said, "this is still a bold color choice."

Hall-Patton said quilters assume this antique Four-Patch is from the 1970s, "but they're off by 130 years."

She may not have much room left at home, either.

"Mark thinks we now have more than 300 quilts in the house," Hall-Patton said, but pointed out "this is also including quilt tops."

Sitting on a bench at the Clark County Museum as the sun set over Henderson, Hall-Patton continued doing the math. "We have maybe eight to 12 family quilts from both sides, and others from friends' families when no one wanted some nice 1930s applique."

There are a few oddities, too: a rare Amish wall-hanging; a Lakota Sundance quilt; a boudoir quilt from the 1930s; and a hand-pieced Four-Patch made entirely out of double-knit. (It's king-sized.)

These quilts came into Hall-Patton's life because on some level they made her happy. If they didn't necessarily do it for her visually — some of those double-knit quilts only a mother could love — the quilts provided direction for her as an anthropologist.

"[American folklorist] William Bascom noted how art offers a particularly useful view of what is occuring in a given culture at a specific time, a condensed version of the society," Hall-Patton said. "Quilts are a way of understanding so many facets of social life through a concentrated lens."

CLOCKWISE FROM UPPER LEFT: At the Clark County Museum, a tie quilt likely made by Nevadan Leva Beckley (ca. 1910); muted colors in Beckley's quilt; professor Hall-Patton expounds on material culture.

ABOVE: At the Clark County Museum, a blue-and-white quilt (ca. 1800) from the Hunsaker-Morrison collection. **OPPOSITE:** Hall-Patton said her *Order Out of Chaos* quilt began in 1980, but wasn't completed until 2010 on account of her "not knowing what [she] was doing."

Clark County Museum administrator and *Pawn Stars* celebrity Mark Hall-Patton steps in to help show *Sunbeam*, a quilt his wife made from a vintage Ruby McKim pattern in 1992.

Hall-Patton has been able to connect scholarly dots for those perhaps unfamiliar with the study of "material culture": the anthropological method of studying physical objects such as tools, art, and written records as a way to understand the culture that produced them. Moreover, she has shown that quilts can be one of the *best* objects a material culture scholar could study. Hall-Patton has done this in her role as a college professor, and as the author of mountains of widely published papers that give quilts the rigorous research they deserve.

The professor is winding down some of her teaching so that she can take up quilt-related research again, since over the years her sociological interests have shifted. (Topics she'd love to investigate: quilts featured in the 1984 Broadway musical *Quilters*, and a potential connection between Cathedral Windows quilts and Korean carrying cloths in the early 20th century.) The other hope is that with a lighter schedule she'll get to make quilts again.

When asked if she thought being a quiltmaker herself added a layer of depth and insight as a quilt scholar, she nodded.

"Absolutely. Knowing how to quilt gave me entree to groups like the Salvation Army Day Home League that was part of my M.A. research ... But I would say that the time spent *with* quilters and just sort of being a fly on the wall meant more."

There was a similar "fly on the wall" approach to Hall-Patton's last academic work, *The Celebrification of a Pawn Star*. The inspiration and case study was her husband, Mark Hall-Patton. Since 2010, Hall-Patton has starred as a celebrity expert on the

History Channel's popular *Pawn Stars*, a show with an audience of millions.

Despite all her credentials and time spent writing down library book call numbers, Hall-Patton is warm and affable with a "just roll with it" personality. Maybe it's time spent in Nevada's 240 days of sunshine; maybe it's her family's crazy-fun *Pawn Stars* experience. Whatever the cause, the affability surfaces in the titles of some of her papers, like one from 2016 entitled *Wait, What? Modern Quilting Existed in the 1950s?*

"I feel like I've spent my life either explaining sociology-slash-anthropology to quilters or quilters to sociologists," the prof said, tucking a piece of hair behind a freckled ear. "The academic stuff can seem *too* academic ... My role models are Barbara Brackman and Jean Ray Laury, [researchers] able

to get very complex ideas across in a way that's approachable." She added that if a person is interested in sticking a toe into quilt studies, "start with Barbara's work, then delve deeper into the academic stuff."

You could also sit in on one of Hall-Patton's Sociology of Art classes at the University of Nevada-Las Vegas; quilts come up every so often in the class she's been teaching since 1999.

"In that class, I have a place to talk about quilts as being important for talking about women's lives," Hall-Patton said. She also uses Baltimore Album construction to explain to her students about the importance of hands-on work. "I pull it in in those ways," she said. Then, with a smile: "I give them fair warning."

BY **Riane Menardi Morrison**

Vegas Strong

A GUILD ANSWERS
THE CALL

On the first day of October in 2017, tragedy struck Las Vegas. A crowd of thousands, gathered for a music festival on the Strip, found themselves running for their lives from an active shooter, open-firing on the crowd. Nearly 60 people were killed. Hundreds were wounded. And Vegas was in shock.

"I think initially it was unreal, like we couldn't even comprehend what really occurred," said Hayle McClellan, president of the Las Vegas Modern Quilt Guild (LVMQG) at the time. McClellan said the only way she can describe the aftermath is to say that that there was "a quiet stillness."

In the days immediately following the tragedy, McClellan and a small group of quilters met at a restaurant. They wanted to be with friends and they wanted to find a way to help. "Our town was hurting, our whole nation was hurting," McClellan said. "We knew we had to do something."

TOP: A few LVMQG members with quilts for their community, including one (center) made for the Vegas Strong Resiliency Center. **BOTTOM:** Haley McClellen and Sue Greene, 2020 guild president.

ABOVE: Modern patchwork, free-motion quilting, and a city shout-out. OPPOSITE: Many quilts made for the Quilts For Vegas drive utilized a Cluck Cluck Sew pattern; all quilts included at least one heart.

Her 50 guildmates were eager to assist in any way they could. The rest of the city was feeling the same way. "Las Vegans just started pouring out from their hearts," McClellan said. "And as we started our healing process, we did what quilters do best — we started sewing."

That fall, the guild was midway through a block lottery, sewing up a modern Log Cabin variation using a block designed by Allison Harris. The block ("Grayscale") was fun, quick, and stash-friendly. McClellan said the group had already made "tons and tons" of blocks, so she simply asked them to keep going. From those blocks they could make quilts for those affected by the tragedy.

Guild members began the project immediately, and chose to include a special detail in each quilt: "We asked that each quilt have at least one heart in it," McClellan said, "so when folks got their quilts, they knew that they were wrapped in love from our community."

The LVMQG sent out a call for donations: Blocks, tops, quilts, and fabric and batting would be accepted and distributed to the community. "Stuff started pouring in the next week, like, immediately," McClellan said.

McClellan received dozens of donations at the elementary school where she worked. As donations came in, she and her students opened each box.

ABOVE: Detail of a guild quilt that won two ribbons at the Desert Quilters of Nevada show in 2016. **OPPOSITE:** At the home of guild member Cathy Eisenzimer (center), a few LVMQG quilters stand strong.

"It's so much more than giving a blanket.
It's pieced with love, it's quilted with love, it's bound with love."

— HAYLE MCCLELLAN, LAS VEGAS MODERN QUILT GUILD

"They loved getting the packages, hearing where they came from, and seeing what came in," McClellan said. "We kept a coloring chart of the states, and every time we got one from a new state, they could color in that state on their chart."

The guild collected around 300 quilts, and the students were able to color the nation. The LVMQG then coordinated with the Vegas Strong Resiliency Center, an organization that provides services and referrals to those affected by the shooting, to distribute the quilts.

"The Resiliency Center was in awe that people cared this much to put together this project," McClellan said. "It's so much more than giving a blanket. It's pieced with love, it's quilted with love, it's bound with love."

On the first anniversary of the shooting, the Resiliency Center began another quilt drive, distributing quilts to those who requested them with a lottery system. The LVMQG was there to help, and they continue making blocks and quilts for those affected.

"What I learned through this is, as much as people hear 'Vegas,' they don't think it's a strong community of people who are caring and giving and willing to help out their neighbor," McClellan said. "But it is. It's a community that really cares."

BY **Riane Menardi Morrison**

Rosillis Rosario
Y LAS FLORES HERMOSAS

———————

Out on the back patio of her pretty Las Vegas home, Rosillis Rosario had the biggest smile on her face. In her native Spanish, her name is pronounced "Ro-zee-es," but our host insisted we call her "Rosie."

The cheerful quilter's name is perfectly suited to the quilts she makes, nearly all of which are adorned with flowers, vines, leaves, and other motifs from nature. Rosario's fabric stash is filled with floral prints that she fussy cuts for appliqué. When she showed us her worktable, we saw that a hand-traced vine motif had been set aside for a future project. Even the shirt "Rosie" chose for our visit was embellished with bright and winsome flowers.

"I love anything that has to do with nature," Rosario said in Spanish as her doting husband, Angel, translated. "Being part of nature, flowers are one of my favorites. I love the colors."

"Rosie" Rosario and a special quilt, characteristically festooned with *flores hermosas* — beautiful flowers.

On these pages, a quilt in progress. Rosario says she uses freezer paper to create her appliqué flowers and each block usually takes about a week to complete.

ABOVE: Details of the quilt Rosario made to commemorate the anniversary of her marriage to Angel. **OPPOSITE:** Angel and Rosie Rosario with a recent creation titled *Medley So Luminous*. **NEXT PAGE:** Detail, *Roses for My Mother* (2016).

Rosie Rosario was born in Costa Rica, a land lush with floral splendor. She learned to make quilts from her mother when she was seven. Rosario says her mother sewed dresses for women and children in the local community. When she turned 18, Rosario moved to New York City with her mother. She almost instantly found Angel.

"We met in my dad's liquor store," her husband said. "She had just arrived to the United States and she walked in the store with her mother. We started dating in May, and we were married seven months later."

This year, they'll celebrate 50 years of marriage.

Rosie and Angel built a life together, moving from New York to California, then Florida, before settling in Nevada. In the early 2000s, they discovered the wide world of quilts together. One day, while flipping through TV channels, Rosario came across an episode of Eleanor Burns's how-to program. She was fascinated. "I like to sew with my hands, and I was doing work like that," Rosario said. "But then

I was watching a quilt show and *that* really caught my attention."

Eleanor Burns became an unofficial teacher. The committed student self-taught her way to impeccable hand appliqué by watching Burns's television shows and using her books. And once she began, Rosario hasn't stopped quilting since.

"I quilt every day," she said. "I never stop."

Soon after Rosario made her first quilt, the couple went to a quilt show in Florida, where they were living at the time. The show was small, and Angel encouraged his wife to enter. "I said to her, 'Look at this. You can do this. You can enter a contest. What you're doing is better than what's in the show.'"

The rookie quilter didn't believe she could compete, but her husband insisted she should try. Eventually, Rosario entered a quilt into a show in Jacksonville, Florida — and she took third place.

Rosario was on cloud nine. She said that it felt so good to win that first award it made her want to enter every single quilt she had ever made into shows.

ABOVE: Rosillis Rosario, an expert quilter with a whole lot of heart. OPPOSITE: In the master bedroom, *Twenty Baskets Full of Flowers*, made in 2020.

Since that first entry, every single quilt that Rosario has made *has* won an award — a feat most quilters can only dream of. She estimates that she's made 20 to 25 quilts since then, averaging one to two per year. "And now I'm retired and I'm making more," she said. "The whole day, quilting."

It wasn't long before Rosario's quilts started winning ribbons — and not as consolation prizes, but for major awards. She can count four that have brought home prestigious "Best of" awards, including *Roses for My Mother,* which won Best of Show at World Quilt Florida 2017. It was a particularly meaningful moment.

"Las rosas para mi mama," Rosario said ("Roses are for my mother.") "Ella amaba las rosas." ("She loved roses.")

When they lived in California, her mother used to grow the biggest flowers in the neighborhood, some measuring as large as 10 inches wide. Today, the Rosarios are trying to grow their own roses in the arid Nevada climate, but to no avail. So the sewing studio serves as a quiltmaker's flower bed, and the roses live on in the quilts.

Rosie and Angel have made quilting a joint venture. Angel drives to the fabric store and he takes photos of all his wife's finished quilts. They pick out fabrics together.

"What else do we do together?" Angel thought for a moment. "We attend the shows. We shop together in the shows. We look at every single quilt there is in there."

To celebrate their anniversary in 2008, Rosie made Angel a special gift: a Baltimore Album–style quilt impeccably appliquéd with a bride and groom in the center and — naturally — gorgeous baskets full of flowers.

It was clear Rosie loves Angel as much today as she did when they met, expressed in the motif that shows up in her quilts again and again: "Me encanta los baskets con flores."

BY **Mary Fons**

Christa Watson
MARATHON RUNNER

———————

Christa Watson could hear her footfalls on the trail. Her breath came heavy as she leaned into the hill that rose up behind the houses in her sleepy Las Vegas neighborhood. Her husband, Jason, wasn't far behind. They were both trying to beat their best time in a favorite race: a nighttime half-marathon. If they pushed hard enough, they could afford to pause — briefly — at the top of the hill to get a clear view of downtown Las Vegas glittering in the valley below like a bowl of sparkling diamonds.

Watson is the first to tell you it's been a long time since she enjoyed that mountain view: She's been too busy running her business.

Christa Watson with husband Jason at their home,
aka "the Quilt House," in Las Vegas.

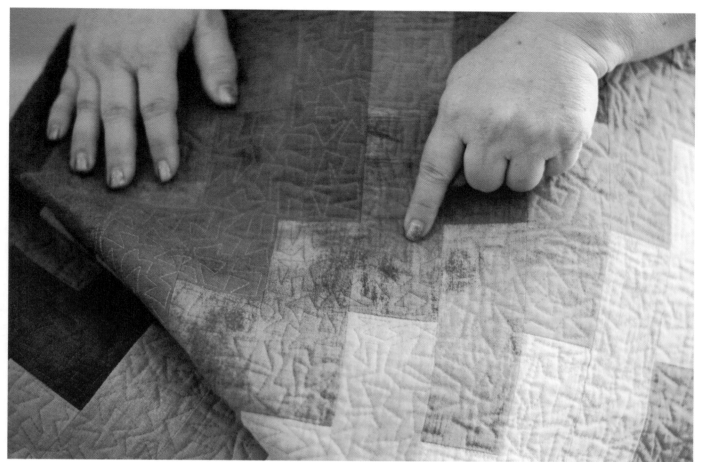

ABOVE: Watson made *Rainbow ZigZags* in 2016 to try quilting a free-motion texture using a different thread color on each fabric.
OPPOSITE: Entrepreneur, mom, wife, and marathon runner Christa Watson.

Mile-a-minute

Christa Watson is the first to tell you lots of things. When you meet her — and plenty of quilters do, at shows, in her workshops, at guild meetings across Nevada — once the conversation begins, it stops for nothing. Watson's natural state is one of breathless excitement; she'll chat about anything under the sun until the sun goes down. But her favorite topic is quilts and her marathon run into the national commercial quilt world.

Watson, who doesn't walk so much as bounce, ushered us into the Las Vegas house she and her husband bought a year ago. The move was easy, since their new, larger home is only a few blocks away from the old one. Watson explained the upgrade.

"There are more bedrooms to use for work. It was cheaper to get a bigger house than rent a separate warehouse. We had a bigger backyard before, but the kids are older now, and —" she smiled as she opened the door to her oldest son's room, "there's more room for merch."

Does Watson's young adult son, home temporarily after a mission trip, mind that his bedroom has been colonized by his parents' commercial operation?

His mother quickly supplied the answer: "We're giving him a super good deal."

The master bedroom hasn't been spared, either: Eight-foot-tall shelves on either side of a window hold more than 50 of Watson's original quilts. Several more were laid out on the bed. Watson said that about 20 of her quilts are out touring at any given time, which is good news for the bedroom.

ABOVE: Quilts by Christa Watson. OPPOSITE: Included in the Modern Quilt Guild's 2017 book, *Modern Quilts: Designs of the New Century*, Watson's *HST Remix* quilt in the master bedroom. PREVIOUS PAGE: Fabric strips from Watson's 2020 fabric line "Good Vibes" (Benartex) and mini-quilt *Abacus* (2014.)

"I mean, we have to sleep in it," she said, sighing. It was hard to tell if Watson's impatience was due to wanting more storage space or because she'd prefer not to sleep at all.

Watson's quilt career marathon began in the mid-90s when the then-20-something coed made her first quilt. Shortly thereafter, she was teaching at a local shop. Two-and-a-half decades of steady cutting, sewing, and pressing has made Watson very good at what she does, though some may not realize just *how* good. Watson came on the scene in 2013, placing her at the tail-end of the first wave of modern quilters, a group who will be the first to admit they were first known for style, not technique. Because of that modern influence, Watson's quilts are largely made with simple shapes and bright colors, hallmarks of the modern style. But Watson had brought serious sewing and quiltmaking skills to the table — even if she didn't know there *was* a table back then.

Watson had been teaching traditional-style quiltmaking for 15 years. She made traditional quilts too; it was all she (or anyone else) really knew. As much as she loved them, "None of those quilts ever fit my house," she said. "I was teaching people to quilt, but those quilts weren't *me.*"

Then came Watson's epiphany: "In 2012, I saw my very first modern quilt. My heart started thumping. My heart's *pounding.* I'm like, 'Where has this been all my life?'"

On these pages, Watson's first modern-style quilt was also the first quilt she submitted to a magazine; *Charming Chevrons* was featured on the cover of *Quilty* magazine in 2013.

ABOVE: Watson in her sunny studio. OPPOSITE: On the design wall, a quilt using her *Good Vibes* fabric collection.

The modern quilt style was what Watson was craving aesthetically, and it "opened the floodgates," as she put it. She spent the next year devouring everything she could find about this new style of quilt.

"I heard about this QuiltCon show," she said. "I'd never been to a national quilt show before, but I just knew I had to go. And I went."

She didn't know a soul at the first-ever QuiltCon (held in Austin, Texas, in 2013) but she left with friends and future colleagues, including modern superstars Angela Walters and Jacquie Gering. These and other professional quiltmakers, many of whom were also in their 30s and 40s, modeled for Watson that she didn't have to walk her career along; she could run.

"I always had something in me [telling me], 'I'm not allowed to do this professionally because I'm not old enough,'" Watson said. "'I can teach locally, but I can't submit to a magazine or go to Road To California.' Who was telling me that? I was telling myself that. QuiltCon allowed me to see that there were other quilters like me and I could do it *now*. I didn't have to retire or wait till my kids were grown to do this."

Today, in addition to the online store (which we know is big enough to warrant the purchase of a new house), Watson has published three books and designs fabric for Benartex. And that show that started it all for her continues to play a role in her life: She teaches and lectures at QuiltCon and has had a quilt in the juried show every year since 2014.

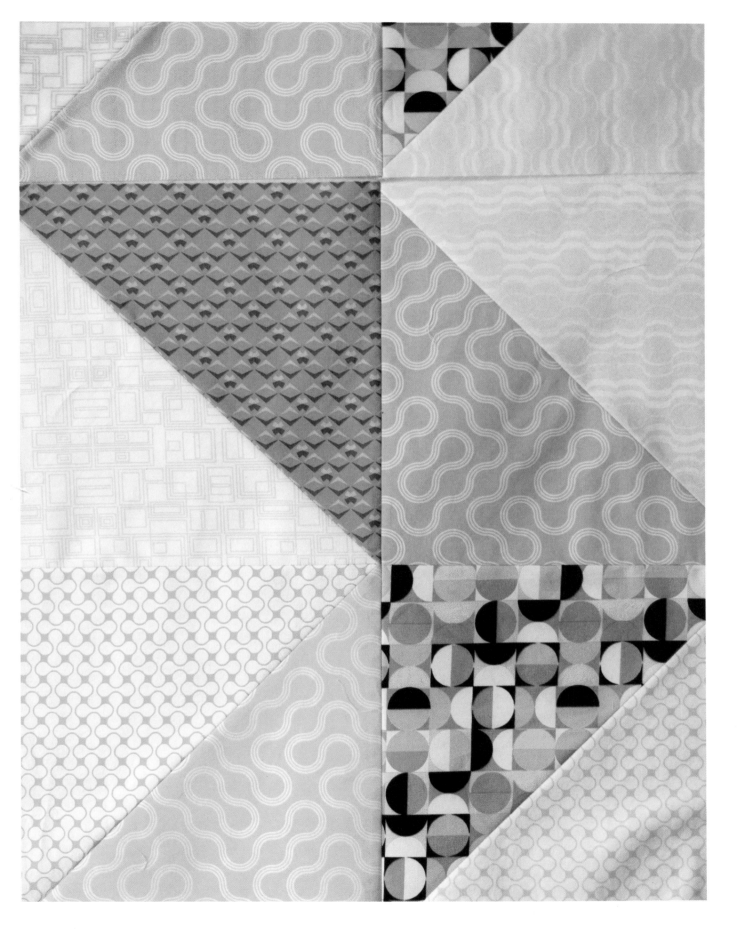

ABOVE: Watson makes mini-quilts to explore thread choices and quilting ideas before making a full quilt; she also uses the finished quilts as samples in her workshops. **OPPOSITE:** Quilts made by Watson between 2016 and 2019 to showcase how machine quilting works on solid or printed fabric.

Christa's choice

Non-quiltmakers often imagine that quilts are made by a group of women sitting around a frame, chatting as they stitch. Those of us who actually make quilts know the process is not done by committee. Yes, there are guilds and retreats, classes and shows. But most quilts are made by one person, in a room, alone, pushing thread through fabric. Quiltmaking is quiet. And whether or not we're conscious of it, lifelong quiltmakers have discovered this and guard that still, quiet place; it's one of the central reasons we make quilts at all.

Anyone who's paying attention can see that past Watson's whirlyball energy, past the conversations that gallop away, she values that quiet place as much as any quilter, maybe more. Because five years ago, Watson realized she was spending her days managing the business and hardly ever making quilts. More than anything she wanted to sew again. With that, she and Jason decided to pull her back from running the show so that she could walk back over to her sewing machine for a different kind of marathon: An all-night sewing session with a clear view of Las Vegas glittering in the distance. 𝒬𝒻

ON THE CUTTING TABLE

As we wrap up Issue 15, so many of the wonderful images
we captured did not make it into the featured stories.
Here are just a few of our favorites. Thank you to everyone who
shared their stories and spaces with us.

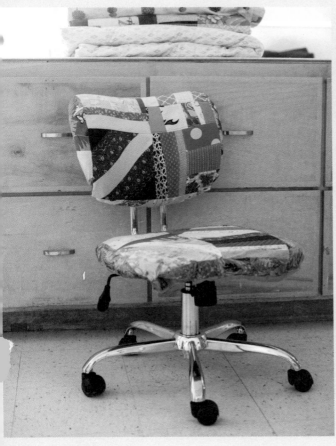

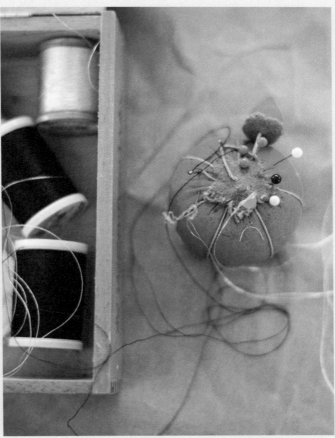

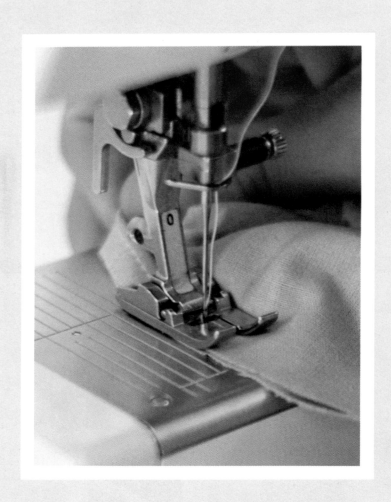